EASY HANDLING

by
Perry Wood

Illustrations by
Carole Vincer

KENILWORTH PRESS

First published in Great Britain by
Kenilworth Press Limited,
Addington, Buckingham, MK18 2JR

British Library Cataloguing in Publication Data
A catalogue record for this book is available from the British Library

ISBN 1-872119-88-3

Printed in Great Britain by Halstan & Co. Ltd

Disclaimer of Liability
The author and publisher shall have neither liability nor
responsibility to any person or entity with respect to any loss or
damage caused or alleged to be caused directly or indirectly by the
information contained in this book. While the book is as accurate as
the authors can make it, there may be errors, omissions and
inaccuracies.

CONTENTS

INTRODUCTION

Handling horses is a necessary and rewarding part of horsemanship. Good handling makes horses safer to be around and can help you to develop a wonderful bond with these beautiful creatures.

It is good to train horses to be easy to handle, but at some time or other most horse-people find they have difficulties handling a horse from the ground, so it is good to learn the skills needed to deal with situations effectively if things go wrong.

Generally speaking, horses that are well-mannered and obedient to handle are more likely to be so when ridden. Of course, there are exceptions to the rule, but the more you make every moment count when you are handling horses from the ground, the closer you will be to having a mutually respectful relationship.

Horses are much bigger, faster and stronger than us, so it is important to establish good habits in our horses and in ourselves to make things easier, safer and more fun for us and for them. The good habits that we need to adopt include things like noticing what horses are telling us, using common sense, acting with good timing and setting sensible boundaries that horses understand.

PRINCIPLES

Once we see things from the horse's point of view, handling problems are often far easier to understand and resolve. Horses see the world in an entirely different way to us: they are a prey animal, which means their instinct is to run away from anything they are unsure about. If they cannot run away, they will instinctively try to protect themselves by kicking out, biting or barging with their body weight.

The instinct to survive is very near the surface in horses and shows itself often in their behaviour. Horses become easier to handle by training or 'conditioning' them. However, even with the best training in the world there is no guarantee a horse's instincts will not show themselves at times!

To teach horses to be easy to handle, you have to be patient and calm, consistent and kind, clear but firm, and see everything from the horse's point of view.

Some horses learn more quickly than others, and some are more nervous about being handled, so it is up to us to give each horse the time and training it needs in order to trust us and become easy to handle.

Horses can be dangerous, so if a horse is too difficult for you to handle, it is best to seek the help of a good professional, for your own benefit as well as the horse's.

LEADING

Leading is an essential part of the horse's training. A horse that leads well usually ties up well, accepts the bridle, doesn't barge into your space, bite, pull or be lazy when ridden and will probably load well too.

Leading a horse is a great way to develop communication, and you can tell a lot about a horse by the way it leads.

It is a good idea, especially with a horse that is not easy to lead, to have a 12-foot (4m) long rope and to wear gloves. The 12-foot rope gives you more space to stay out of the way if the horse leaps or rears yet still allows you to hold onto him.

Ideally you want to lead a horse with some slack in the rope. You want him to walk at your speed and stop when you stop. When you lead a horse, walk at your own pace and in a definite direction, so it is clear to him where you are both going and at what speed. It's a good idea to teach him to be led from the right as well as the left side.

> **Avoid holding the horse too tightly on the rope: he will feel restricted and be more inclined to pull to escape the tightness.**

Practise training the horse to lead with you at his shoulder, the girth area and next to his head. If you can lead a horse easily in all of those positions, you know he is listening and accepting your guidance.

If a horse drags behind – without looking around at the horse, give a gentle forward feel on the rope and then tap him behind with a schooling stick. **Or if he stands and won't move** – lead his head and shoulders sideways, then once he starts moving his feet, ask him to come forwards.

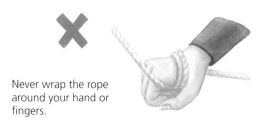

Never wrap the rope around your hand or fingers.

If a horse is inattentive, use intermittent vibrations or shakes on the rope to bring his head around to look at you: as soon as he looks your way, let the rope go slack and motionless. Repeat this process each time he looks away.

If intermittent vibrations or shakes on the rope don't get his attention, hold the rope into your body with both hands and turn back on yourself, walking determinedly in the opposite direction so that he has to swing around to follow you – see below.

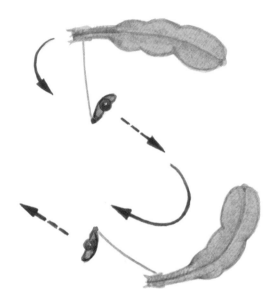

If a horse pulls strongly ahead of you – hold the rope firmly with both hands and plant your feet, so that the horse 'bumps' into a solid feel on the halter and stops. (Horses are much stronger than humans, so it is more effective for him to bump himself to a stop on the rope than for you to try pulling him to stop.) Once the horse has stopped, continue walking and repeat the process each time he gets strong or pulls ahead of you.

Keep turning this way and that every few steps so that he has to pay attention to you in order to keep up with your changes of direction.

If a horse barges into you – turn his head slightly TOWARDS YOU (it is more difficult for a horse to barge you with his shoulder if his head is facing you), make sure the rope is long enough for him to be away from you and poke him intermittently with the point of your elbow on his shoulder or chest; without looking him in the eye, shouting or getting annoyed.

CATCHING A HORSE IN THE FIELD

Horses that are hard to catch can be very frustrating to deal with. The important thing is to figure out why a horse doesn't want to be caught. How does he view the experiences he has with people? What happens to him when he is caught? Does he have to do lots of hard work he doesn't enjoy? Does he have an unpleasant time? How could the time he spends around people be made more pleasurable for him so he not only lets himself be caught, but also looks forward to being caught and even starts 'catching himself'?

When you go to catch a horse, walk in a confident and casual manner; don't go creeping up or marching in.

Holding the halter behind your back is not a good idea: horses are suspicious creatures and they're not silly – they can see you're hiding something.

Offering food as an incentive is often effective, but is a quick-fix solution, because when you next go to catch the horse without food he may not be willing to oblige.

Horses are herd animals and their behaviour is affected by each other, so it is a good idea to know all the horses in the field and how they get along. Find out who is friends with whom, who is the leader, which horses are bullies and which get picked on. Even if you don't know all this, whenever you go to catch a horse that is turned out with others, watch the other horses to see what is going on between them.

It is best to turn horses out in company; horses standing out on their own all the time can develop mental or behavioural problems, because they are naturally sociable creatures and being on their own upsets them.

Does your horse associate being caught with good, or bad, experiences?

If there are other horses crowding around the horse you are going to catch, be aware that they could run into you or squash you without meaning to. Pick a suitable space to approach the horse, lower your eyes and walk in a manner that suggests you are going to walk past him, then approach him with your body turned slightly at an angle away from him and your eyes looking away from him. Rub his neck in a way that is pleasurable for him and casually slip the halter over his nose or the rope over his neck, then do up the halter. All the time, be

When catching a horse, always be aware of the other horses in the field, and of what is going on between them.

aware of what the other horses are doing.

If your horse runs away when you try to catch him, don't chase after him, shout or get annoyed, just smile and quietly walk after him with the attitude that you have all the time in the world and that you *know* he'll give in before you do.

If he is more difficult to catch, you could try standing between him and the rest of the horses, stopping him from joining the herd.

If things are really tough, you may need to take all other horses out of the field, so the one you want is left on his own with you, at which point he may soon want to be with someone, even if that someone has a halter in their hands!

It makes sense to keep a horse that is hard to catch in a smaller paddock until he becomes easier. Another idea is to leave a breakable halter on him, with a 1–2 foot (30–60cm) piece of rope hanging.

It is good practice to set up a routine where you catch your horse, feed him and turn him out without doing any work. Or a

routine of going to him in the field, stroking him, then going away again without catching him, so he learns he is not going to be worked every time he sees you. Have a really good think about how you could ride and work the horse in ways he enjoys, so he looks forward to being caught.

Turning a horse out in a breakable halter, with a 1–2ft (30–60cm) piece of rope hanging, can make catching easier.

TYING UP

It is important to train horses to tie up well for grooming, shoeing, etc. A horse that leads well and follows the feel of the halter will usually tie up well.

Tie horses up to something safe and strong, such as a wall, rather than a flimsy post or fence. Tie the lead rope to a loop of baler twine or string attached to a tie-ring – the loop will break in an emergency, e.g. if the horses panics, pulls back and falls to the ground.

If a horse panics while tied up, remain calm yourself: if he breaks free, he less likely to bolt off if you stay calm.

Never tie a horse somewhere unfamiliar and leave him unattended: make sure he feels safe and comfortable. Ideally choose a spot where he can see other horses while they are being groomed, shod, etc.

Never tie a horse up by the bridle or reins.

Quick-release knot

In an emergency, this knot can be undone by pulling on the end of the rope. Practise this knot until tying it becomes second-nature.

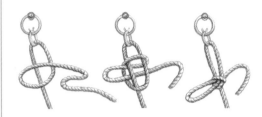

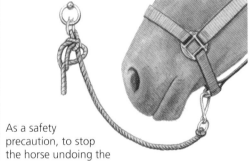

As a safety precaution, to stop the horse undoing the knot with his teeth, pass the end of the rope through the loop.

Always tie your horse to something solid, safe and strong - not to something that he can pull down or move.

Tying horses low down or with the rope so long they can get their front legs over the rope is dangerous. Gates do not make sensible tying places either.

Pulling back when tied up

Horses that pull back can hurt themselves, as well as being an inconvenience to handle. If a young horse has been taught to lead and respond well to the halter, it will usually accept being tied up, but some horses learn that by pulling back they can get away.

If a horse has ever pulled back at some time in its life, it may have frightened itself so much that it panics and pulls back whenever it is tied up.

No method is a cure-all for this problem, but you may wish to try the technique illustrated below (which can also be used when teaching a horse to accept being tied up).

Use a longish rope and instead of tying the horse, simply pass the rope through the tie-ring while you hold the other end. When the horse pulls back, give him more rope by allowing it to pass through the ring, then quietly encourage him to step forwards from behind and gently bring the rope back through the ring. This usually prevents him panicking because he doesn't feel the tight pull on the end of the rope. In time may feel safer about being tied.

Teaching a horse to accept being tied up or retraining one that pulls back habitually. If the horse pulls back, release the pressure by feeding the rope through the tie-ring.

Once the horse is calm, gently encourage him to step forward while taking up the slack in the rope.

> **The more you can do to make the horse feel safe about being tied up, the better.**

RESPECTING YOUR SPACE

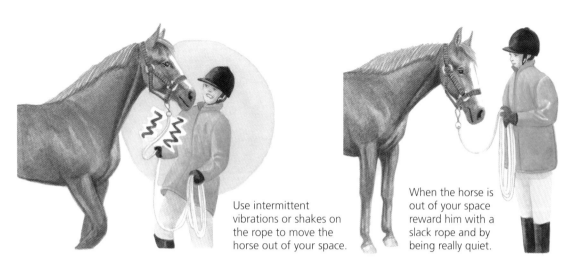

Use intermittent vibrations or shakes on the rope to move the horse out of your space.

When the horse is out of your space reward him with a slack rope and by being really quiet.

Horses that barge or crowd your space can be difficult to handle and, in the worse cases, dangerous. Horses and ponies weigh an average of half a ton and if they bump into you they can knock you down, squash you against walls or doorways or stand on your feet, without even knowing they are doing it! So it is important to teach horses to respect your body space. To do that means having a good idea about how much space you want to have between you and the horse, and most importantly it means being consistent and sticking to that rule all the time.

Horses in a herd naturally bunch up close together when they feel anxious; they also bump into each other as a way of expressing dominance over one another. So horses are most likely to crowd you when they are upset or fearful, or when they want to dominate you. At these times it is not so easy to deal with barging, so establish ground rules and teach your horse to respect your space when things are calm.

To avoid being barged make sure the horse is aware that you are there, and have a good idea how much space around you is comfortable – and stick to it! Whenever the horse comes even a tiny bit closer than you want, correct him by moving him back to where you want **him**, using intermittent vibrations and shakes on the lead rope. Some horses try to enter your space in very subtle ways; without actually stepping in your direction you may notice them lean their body towards you. This is their way of testing your boundaries.

Remember that a dominant horse, such as a herd leader, would not allow another

Make yourself larger than life and use your energy and presence to move horses out of your space.

horse into its body space without an invitation, such as for mutual grooming. To be safe, you have to do the same.

Horses that are boisterous and dominate other horses by crowding them are more likely to be the ones that barge and crowd people too. You may have to ask this type of horse to give you more space than usual.

> It is mostly a waste of time having a physical pushing match with a horse to get him out of your space – horses move into physical pressure and are VERY strong. Instead, use intermittent pressure, such as repeated tapping on the horse with your elbow, or shaking the halter rope, to get him to back off.

As with leading, remember that a horse can move his body into your space more easily if his head is turned **away** from you. That means it is best to ask him to turn his head **towards** you.

GROOMING

Some horses can be unhappy about being groomed. Horses are so sensitive they can feel a fly land on their body and flick it off by twitching their skin. So when we groom a horse we must realise just how much they can feel with their skin.

Avoid grooming areas that cause the horse distress unless it is absolutely necessary. For example, if you are riding only to exercise the horse and he is upset about being groomed, perhaps just cleaning the areas where the saddle and bridle fit would suffice. Riding a muddy horse that is happy may be preferable

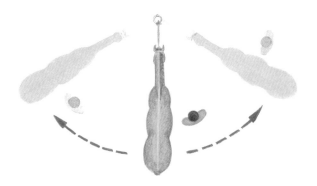

Always tie horses up to be groomed, using a quick-release knot. Choose somewhere which gives you room to step out of the way if a horse starts moving around.

GROOMING CONT.

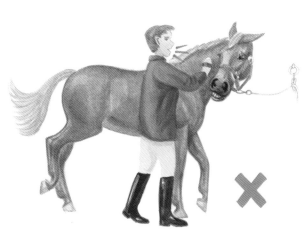

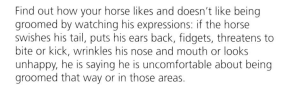

Find out how your horse likes and doesn't like being groomed by watching his expressions: if the horse swishes his tail, puts his ears back, fidgets, threatens to bite or kick, wrinkles his nose and mouth or looks unhappy, he is saying he is uncomfortable about being groomed that way or in those areas.

If the horse looks relaxed and sleepy, lowers his head and rests one back leg, he is saying he is happy to be groomed that way.

to riding one that is spotlessly clean but unhappy.

Make your brush-strokes rhythmical and steady so the horse knows when the next brush-stroke is coming. Brush the horse as you would want to be brushed yourself: be kind, polite and caring.

All horses are different, but many enjoy being groomed on the crest of the neck, forelock, back of the rump and tail. Some horses are unhappy about being groomed under the girth and belly area, on the back, at the tops of the back legs, around the ribs and ears, and sometimes the front of the neck.

A really ticklish horse may benefit from being groomed with a coconut matting glove or your gloved hands, rather than a brush.

A horse that is difficult to groom will gradually improve over time if it is treated with respect and gains trust in the person

doing the grooming. With this kind of horse, it is better always to have the same, caring person grooming the horse, rather than lots of different handlers.

> **Never lose your temper with a horse that is unhappy about grooming.**

For horses that snap or bite, tie them up so they cannot reach you with their teeth, and have your elbow sticking out to one side, so it protects you.

TACKING UP – BRIDLING

If a horse is persistently unhappy about the bridle or bit, have a professional check the teeth. Also make sure the bridle and bit are a good fit for the horse.

To help a horse to be easy to bridle, tie him in a place where he is happy and you can reach his head easily. Avoid holding the bridle in a threatening way. Be gentle and take your time throughout the whole bridling process, as shown in the four steps below.

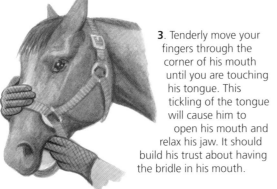

1. Stand on the horse's left, hold his nose with your right hand and softly lower his head, bringing it around towards you slightly. If the horse's head is bent towards you like this, he is less able to throw it in the air. If the horse evades by throwing his head about, keep your hand softly in the same place on his nose and passively follow his head until he stops objecting.

2. If a horse is sensitive around his lips or objects to opening his mouth for the bit, use your left hand to stroke the side of his face and muzzle, then gently insert your fingers into the corner of his mouth. (Do this without the bridle for now.)

3. Tenderly move your fingers through the corner of his mouth until you are touching his tongue. This tickling of the tongue will cause him to open his mouth and relax his jaw. It should build his trust about having the bridle in his mouth.

4. Once you can do this, repeat steps 1, 2 and 3 with the bridle in position in your right hand. Only insert the bit when the horse's mouth and teeth are open wide as a result of your touching his tongue. If his mouth is open enough, you can take your time and slowly insert the bit into his mouth without banging his teeth.

For horses that to move away when you bridle them, try using a headcollar that has a buckle on the nose. Put the bridle on over the top of the headcollar, and then unbuckle the headcollar and slip it out from underneath the bridle.

Always take the bridle off with care. Let the horse lower the bit out of his mouth so it doesn't clank his teeth, otherwise he may be bridle-shy the next time you want to put it on him.

TACKING UP – SADDLING

Have a professional check the suitability and fit of the saddle. You should also have the horse's back checked so you know he is in good shape.

Many horses are sour about being saddled because it was done in an unsuitable or uncomfortable way for them in the past and they remember the bad experience.

Move in a steady and deliberate way, and avoid looking the horse in the eye while saddling him. Carry the saddle towards the horse in a casual, non-threatening way. Stroke the horse's back where saddle is going to go, before placing the saddle gently on his back. Place the saddle quite far forwards towards the withers and slide it back a little into place. Never slide the saddle forwards.

Always do the girth up slowly and gently in at least three stages, perhaps over a period of a few minutes. (Imagine someone tightening a belt around your ribs and under your armpits – that is what the girth is like to a horse.) Let the stirrups down in a gentle way too.

If a horse snaps, bites or cow-kicks at the girth or saddle, it is important to realise he is telling you something: perhaps the girth is too tight, the saddle is hurting his back, or he is sore or worried about being treated too roughly.

If saddling a confirmed biter, tie the horse up and use your elbow to protect yourself, as shown in page 13.

Stroke the horse's back, as though brushing down velvet, before gently placing the saddle on his back.

Do not approach with the saddle in a rough or quick manner as this can upset the horse.

SHOEING AND PICKING UP THE HORSE'S FEET

Picking up horses' feet and shoeing them is contrary to the horse's nature. Horses instinctively use their legs and feet to run away from danger, so to trust a human to hold onto their feet and nail hot iron shoes onto their hooves is asking a lot.

Horse's legs are designed to move backwards and forwards but have very little ability to move out sideways. This means you have to pick the feet up without pulling them out sideways towards you. The front feet should be raised up under the horse's body and the back feet moved out behind the horse, but ideally no higher than the hock joint. Watch an experienced and kind farrier to see how he handles horses' feet in ways that they are comfortable with.

Never grab, use strength or surprise to pick up a horse's feet: it is more likely to make them be difficult. Instead, take your time, be patient and train the horse by making him feel safe about picking his feet up for you.

A horse has to be able to support his weight on the remaining three legs when you pick up a foot.

Use the halter to move him backwards or forwards until he stands in balance before you start. Many horses, especially youngsters, react badly if you attempt to pick up a foot when their other feet are not arranged so they can support themselves properly.

Picking up the horse's feet

It is a good idea to tie a horse up with plenty of space around you, so you can get out of the horse's way if you need to.

If a horse stamps its foot back down, waves it around or does anything else you don't want while tryin to pick up his feet, don't get annoyed, just relax and repeat the process shown right.

If a horse is dangerous and kicking around with his back legs, use a long stick (about 4 ft/1.2m long) perhaps with a stiff gardening glove attached to the end (see page 24), to desensitise the leg. Stroke the legs and feet with it until he stops reacting. Always be persistent and quiet. Once he accepts the stick on his legs and feet, do the same thing with your hand.

Some horses need time and patience in

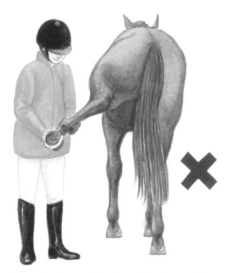

Don't pick up the horse's foot by pulling it out sideways or too high as this can be uncomfortable for the horse.

order to be good about having their feet handled, so quietly work away at this every day as a routine.

Preparation for shoeing

To prepare a horse to be shod, or to re-train a horse that is difficult to shoe, each day do a little of the process described above for picking up the horse's feet. Gradually hold the feet up for longer, begin to tap gently on the underside of the foot, perhaps with a hoof pick, and then put the foot back down.

Over days or weeks, gradually build up the tapping so the horse is comfortable with being tapped for longer and quite hard, as this is what the farrier has to do to shoe the horse. It may be worth borrowing a hammer from the farrier and practising tapping your horse's feet with it until he is relaxed with the feeling.

When the horse is good with you, have other people pick up the horse's feet. Ask the farrier to pick up the horse's feet on visits prior to being shod, so that the horse becomes comfortable with the farrier without having the extra challenge of being shod.

If possible, regularly tie the horse up near the farrier while other horses are being shod, so he gets used to the smells, sights and sounds of shoeing.

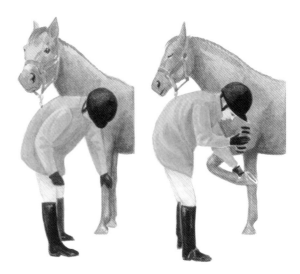

To pick up a front foot correctly, stand facing the back of the horse and use the hand nearest the horse to pick up a foot. Slowly run your hand from the horse's shoulder, down the back of the front leg, to the bottom of the cannon bone, and apply softy increasing pressure until the horse responds by picking up the foot. Hold the raised foot up in a positive and gentle way. Use your spare hand to stroke the horse's leg all over, before placing the foot back on the ground.

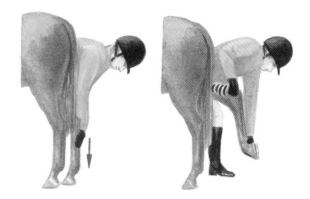

When the horse is comfortable with having the front feet picked up, run your hand from the top of the rump, down a hind leg and follow the same procedure for the hind feet. Hold the hind foot out behind the horse a little, and use your other hand to stroke the leg, before placing the foot back on the ground.

17

LOADING

Horses are claustrophobic creatures and try to run away when they feel threatened, but when they are in a lorry or trailer they cannot escape by running away. This can cause them to be fearful, and it is usually this fear that makes them difficult to load.

A horse that goes happily into a trailer loads his mind as well as his body, which means he has decided for himself that the trailer/lorry is safe. That is the aim for easy handling.

Take the time to *train* the horse to load easily. People often try to load their horse in a hurry on the morning of a show or competition without having trained the horse to load beforehand on stress-free occasions.

When you have sessions training your horse to load, make sure you have lots of time free. If you give the horse all the time he needs, it will be easier because the horse will sense you are relaxed.

Help the horse to feel safe with you when he is near the trailer by being calm and patient yourself. If the handler gets angry or frustrated, the horse will feel threatened and is less likely to cooperate.

Reward the horse by stroking, with soothing words, a rest, a feed or by putting slack in the rope when he does what you want, e.g. goes further onto the ramp. Do not punish him when he does not do what you want, but make sure that you don't unintentionally reward him at those times either!

Tips

- When a horse refuses to move forwards (perhaps only halfway into the trailer) it can be tempting to tap the horse's behind to make him walk on. With trailer loading this can backfire, and rather than the horse going forwards he comes flying back out again! **Only encourage or tap the horse behind when his feet are actually moving him forwards.** This will take him further into the trailer.

- It is sensible to use a 12-foot (4m) long rope when loading. This can help you to hold on to the horse more easily if he moves away from you quickly.

To stop a horse stepping off the sides of the ramp, park the trailer/lorry where there is a wall, bank, hedge or similar barrier on both sides of the ramp to block the horse's option of going out to the side. If you don't have such a place and your horse does go off to the side, notice which way he goes most often and block that side or get an effective horse person to stand on that side.

Pulling forwards strongly on the rope can make a horse throw his head in the air and shoot backwards. Instead, have a gentle, inviting feel on the rope that gives and takes softly. Any time he comes forwards to your inviting 'feel' on the rope, immediately put some slack in the rope as a reward.

Teach your horse to lead well: a horse that leads well should go wherever the person leading asks it to go, and that includes going into a trailer.

If a horse backs down the ramp or away from the trailer insted of loading, rather than getting behind him with a stick or lunge line, try backing him up as though it was your idea to go backwards. Back him away from the trailer a few more steps than he intended to go, and then walk **immediately** forwards, straight back towards the trailer and up the ramp.

Do not try to stop him backing up: if he backs up again, you join in again as though you are asking him to back up and repeat the process as many times as necessary!

Horses will often walk forwards and further up the ramp with each repetition. When the horse has gone a little further than previously, let him pause for a minute or two and stroke him while he stands still.

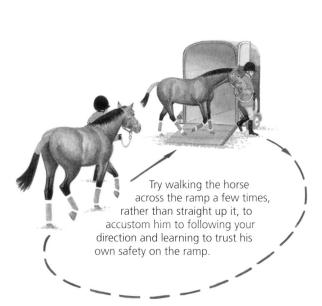

Try walking the horse across the ramp a few times, rather than straight up it, to accustom him to following your direction and learning to trust his own safety on the ramp.

- Open the front door and ramp of the trailer, so the trailer looks less claustrophobic and the horse thinks he can walk straight through.

- Try parking the trailer in the horse's field, with the front and back doors open. Feed the horse each day by placing his bucket near the trailer, then after a few days place it on the ramp, and then eventually inside the trailer, so he identifies the trailer with a positive experience.

- When a horse who has been difficult to load finally goes into the trailer, it can be tempting to slam the door shut quick and feel relieved that he has loaded. Rather

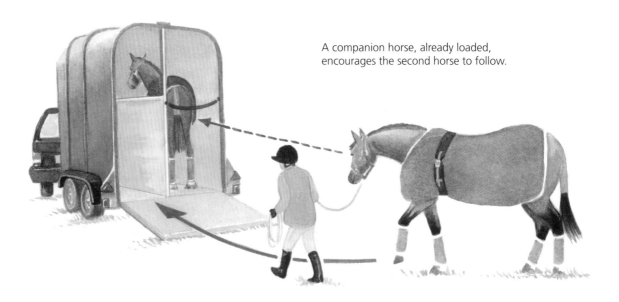

A companion horse, already loaded, encourages the second horse to follow.

than shut him in and start your journey, try stroking him for a minute or two inside the trailer and then lead him out and load him all over again. Repeat this until he loads without hesitation (usually it takes only a few times). It should get easier each time and will probably make him load better on a future occasion, because he will be loading *with his mind* as well as his body.

- To help a horse to be less afraid of the trailer or lorry, stand and wait with him at whatever distance from the trailer he is at ease. Gradually move him a little closer, waiting to make sure he is happy at each stage before moving closer again.

With a horse on board, it is essential that the vehicle be driven carefully. If a horse has a difficult journey because of bad driving, he will not be so willing to travel anywhere next time.

CLIPPING

Many horses in work need to be clipped in the winter months and this can be a problem if the horse is fearful of being clipped. Horses can be afraid of the noise of the clippers, the feeling of the clippers on their body, or because they have been hurt in the past.

Make sure the horse is clean, dry and well groomed and the clipper blades are sharp and adjusted correctly (speak to your supplier about this). If the blades are blunt, not adjusted correctly or get too hot, the horse will have good reason to be unhappy about being clipped.

Tie the horse somewhere safe for you and for him, with good footing and space for you to keep the clipper's electric cable out of the way of the horse's feet.

For horses that are afraid of the noise, try regularly playing a tape of the clipper sound. Experiments have shown that playing the sound every day for a few weeks in the stable-block just before the horses are fed and during the time they eat makes most horses associate the sound with something pleasurable.

Begin by standing between the horse and the clippers and stroke the horse with your spare hand, while running the clippers. When the horse totally relaxes, switch off the clippers. Repeat this process until the horse does not react to the sound at all.

To desensitise the horse even more, stroke him with the clippers whilst they are switched off, until he relaxes. Eventually you should be able to place the back of the hand (the one holding the clippers) on the horse's skin, at first with the clippers switched off, and later, running. This gets the horse used to the feeling of the vibration of the clippers on his body through your hand before clipping commences. Alternatively you could use a battery-operated shaver (they are quieter and don't have cables attached), **not** to clip the horse with, but as a training aid.

As part of getting the horse used to the sound and the buzzing feeling on his body, hold the clippers in your hand, and place the back of the hand on the horse's skin.

Regularly playing the sound of clippers running is a useful way to familiarise horses with the noise of the clippers in a non-threating way.

BITING

Biting can be an established habit for some horses and is not always quick or easy to deal with.

Horses bite for a variety of reasons, but the underlying cause of biting is usually that the horse is afraid or being defensive. Occasionally horses bite to dominate a person, just as they might dominate another horse.

Whatever his reasons for biting, by this behaviour he is trying to tell us something and it will pay us to listen and find out what the horse is unhappy about.

With a biting horse arrange things so you are out of biting range as much as possible. Teach the horse to lead and stand a safe distance from you at all times.

Always tie the horse up to groom and tack him up etc. Tack up and groom with sensitivity, so the horse isn't tempted to bite as a way of defending himself from tactless grooming or rough tacking up.

Never give a biting horse titbits from your hands. Giving titbits by hand can actually be the cause of a biting habit.

Avoid toying with the horse's mouth or head as a way of saying hello to him. You don't need to put your hand near a horse's mouth or let him sniff your hand to greet him.

When a horse bites it can be very tempting to shout or hit the horse, but this can often make matters worse. While hitting a horse may stop it biting that time, it can make the horse quicker and meaner to bite next time.

KICKING

Kicking is usually the result of the horse thinking he needs to defend himself, but whatever the cause, kicking needs to be handled with skill and tact, otherwise you can be hurt or make the horse a more vicious kicker, or both.

It is important to always be aware and respectful around a horse known to kick.

A horse that kicks in the stable can be a real danger. A stable is an unnaturally confining space for a horse, which means he may be more likely to defend himself by kicking out. Get this type of horse to come to the stable door (perhaps for a titbit) and hook a lead rope onto his headcollar so you have hold of his head before entering the stable.

Keep the horse's head toward you at all times. Avoid mucking out, grooming, tacking up, or doing anything else around the horse while he is in the stable; instead take him outside and tie him somewhere safer.

Before entering the stable of a known kicker, attach a lead rope to his headcollar so you have control of the 'front end'.

> **An habitual kicker should be referred to a professional. Remember: if a horse has ever shown a tendency to kick, he may do it again.**

A horse that kicks out at other equines when led or tied on the yard should be kept at a sensible distance from other horses.

> **Remember: horses can cow-kick sideways and forwards as well as kick backwards.**

A horse that kicks out near you when you are catching or leading another horse in the pasture is a real danger and may be dealt with by being 'seen off' with a long stick such as a broom handle. This type of horse is not respecting your presence and is showing dangerously dominant behaviour.

KICKING CONT.

Here is something you can try to help rectify the problem. Tie the horse somewhere safe, with plenty of room for you to step out of the way if he swings round or kicks, and stroke him all over with a stick (about 4 ft/1.2m long). On no account hit the horse with the stick. 'Gentle' the horse by stroking him with the end of the stick, staying out of kicking range at all times. Start with the shoulders and gradually work your way down his body to his legs, so that he learns the touch is safe. If he kicks out or reacts to being stroked on his legs with the stick, quietly persist and keep stroking him until he allows his legs to be touched. Use this method with the stick for as many days as you need to, until he accepts the touch without reacting.

Build trust with a kicker by stroking him gently with a long stick. In time the horse should accept the light touch of the stick all over his body, including the hind legs. Do not hit the horse with the stick as this will lose his trust and may make him kick even more.

CONCLUSION

What a joy it is when a horse is easy to handle and can be taken anywhere. Most horses can be trained to lead well, and be easy to catch, shoe and box. It sometimes takes patience, tact and common sense from us to teach them how we want them to behave around us, and teaching horses to do these things can be a fun and rewarding part of horsemanship.

It is said that 'mean horses are made, not born', and this is basically true, so our job is always to handle horses in a caring and thoughtful way so we raise them to be gentle and well-mannered.

Of course, there are horses that are difficult and dangerous, and if you have a horse like that you must refer it to an expert professional, rather than risking your own safety, as well as the horse's.

Wouldn't it be wonderful to give every horse in the world the opportunity to become easy to handle? Perhaps you can start to give them that opportunity, by always handling the horses you know in a skilful, kind and knowledgeable way.